RUBANK EDUCATIONAL LIBRARY No. 145

Concert
and Contest
COLLECTION

T0079573

for

C FLUTE
with piano accompaniment

Compiled and Edited

by H. VOXMAN

RUBANK®

HAL•LEONARD® CORPORATION
7777 W. BLUEMOUND RD. P.O. BOX 13819 MILWAUKEE, WI 53213

Contents

CONCERT AND CONTEST COLLECTION for Flute

Gavotte

FR. JOS. GOSSEC
Edited by H. Voxman

Copyright Renewed

Copyright MCMXLIX by Rubank, Inc., Chicago, Ill.
International Copyright Secured

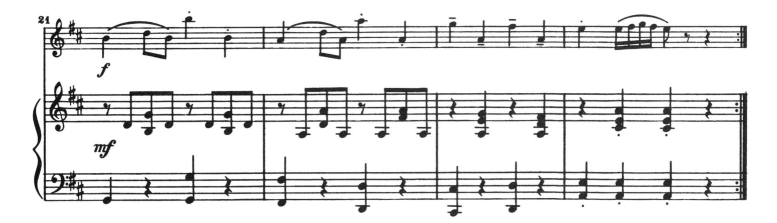

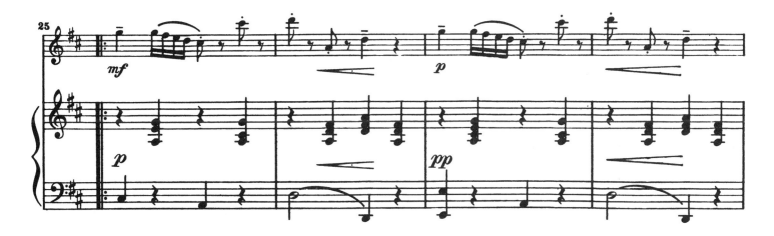

Bergamask

PAUL KOEPKE
Edited by H. Voxman

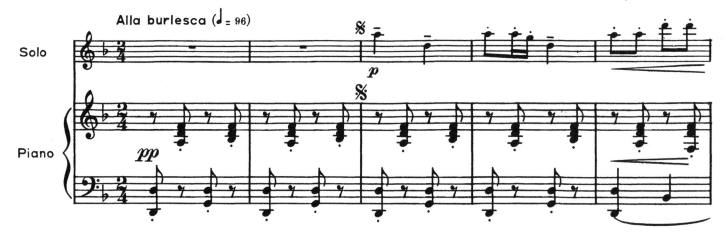

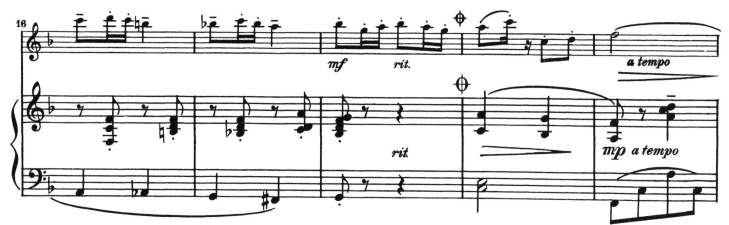

Copyright MCMXLIX by Rubank, Inc., Chicago, Ill.
International Copyright Secured

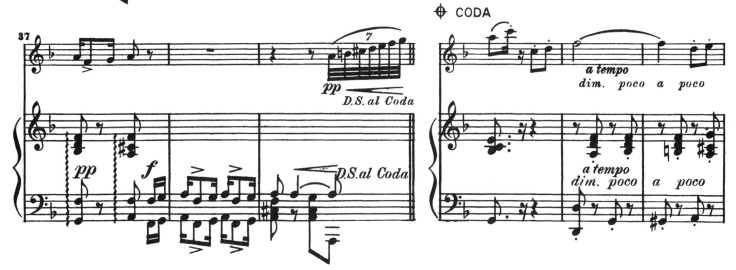

Serenade

VICTOR HERBERT, Op. 3
Edited by H. Voxman

Copyright MCMXLIX by Rubank, Inc., Chicago, Ill.
International Copyright Secured

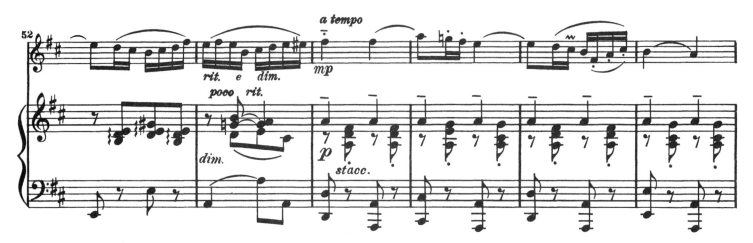

Scherzino

JOACHIM ANDERSEN, Op. 55, No. 6
Edited by H. Voxman

Copyright MCMXLIX by Rubank, Inc., Chicago, Ill.
International Copyright Secured

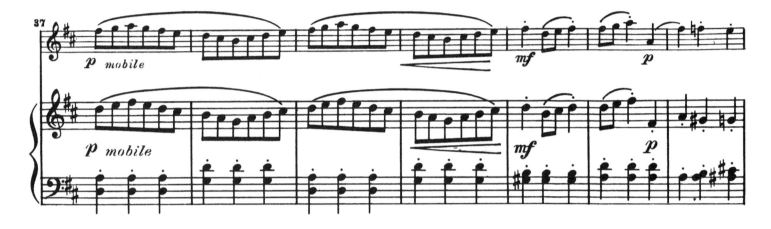

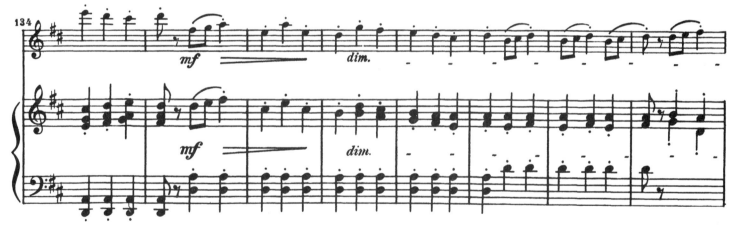

Valse Gracieuse

W. POPP, Op. 261, No. 2
Edited by H. Voxman

Copyright MCMXLIX by Rubank, Inc., Chicago, Ill.
International Copyright Secured

Valse, tempo moderato [in one]

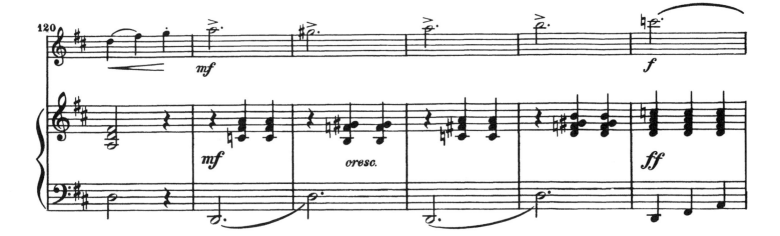

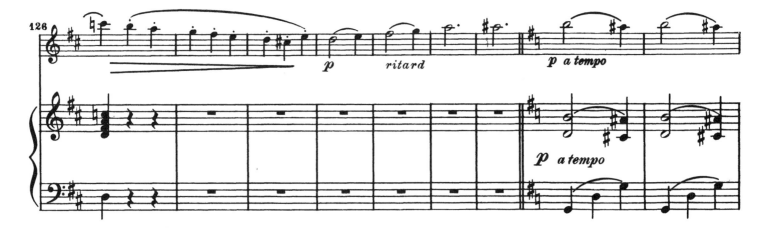

Andalouse

ÉMILE PESSARD, Op. 20
Edited by H. Voxman

Copyright MCMXLIX by Rubank, Inc., Chicago, III.
International Copyright Secured

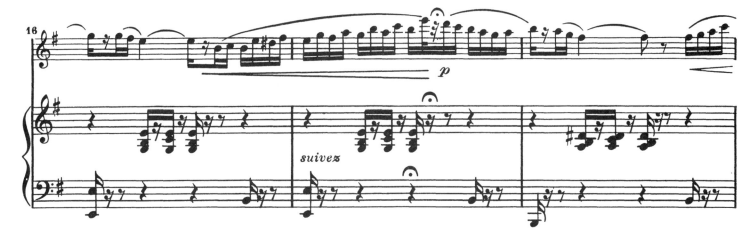

Menuet
from
L'Arlésienne Suite No. 2

GEORGES BIZET
Edited by H. Voxman

Copyright MCMXLIX by Rubank, Inc., Chicago, Ill.
International Copyright Secured

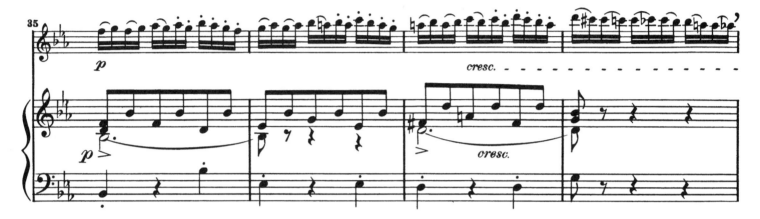

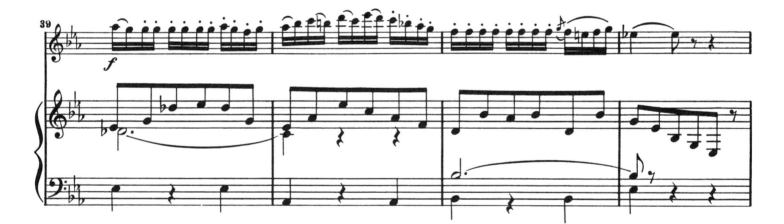

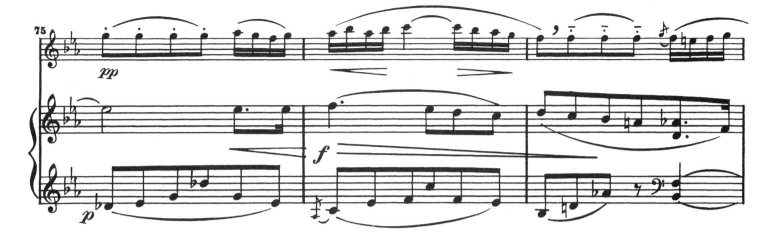

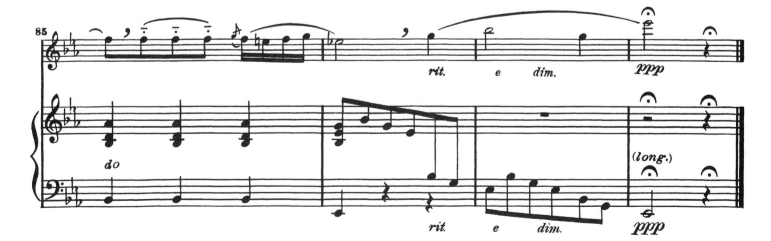

Serenade

JOS. HAYDN
Edited by H. Voxman

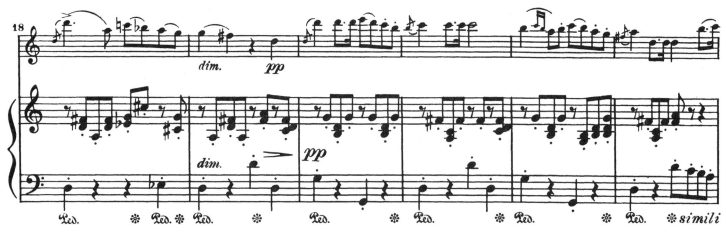

Copyright MCMXLIX by Rubank, Inc., Chicago, Ill.
International Copyright Secured

Siciliana and Giga
from
Sonata V

G. F. HANDEL
Edited by H. Voxman

Copyright MCMXLIX by Rubank, Inc., Chicago, Ill.
International Copyright Secured

Menuet and Spirit Dance

from Orpheus

C. W. von GLUCK
Edited by H. Voxman

Copyright MCMXLIX by Rubank, Inc., Chicago, Ill.
International Copyright Secured

SPIRIT DANCE
Più lento (in 6)

Polonaise and Badinerie
from
Suite in B Minor

J. S. BACH
Edited by H. Voxman

Copyright MCMXLIX by Rubank, Inc., Chicago, Ill.
International Copyright Secured

Trio (Double)

Polonaise D.C. al Fine
(without repeats)

BADINERIE
Presto

Romance

GEORGES BRUN, Op. 41
Edited by H. Voxman

Modéré, sans lenteur
(Moderately, without dragging)

Solo

Piano

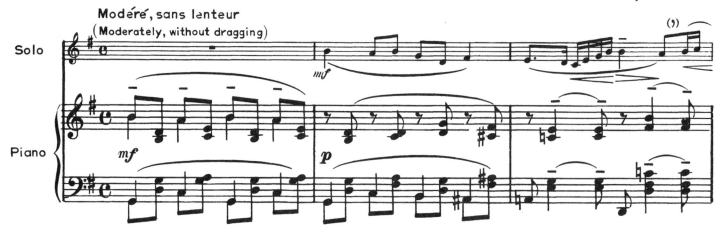

Un peu retenu (a little slower)

Calme

Suivez (follow)

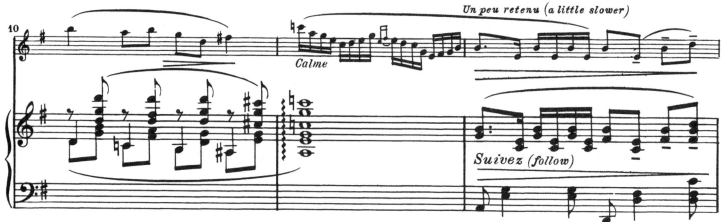

Copyright MCMXLI by Rubank, Inc., Chicago, Ill.
International Copyright Secured

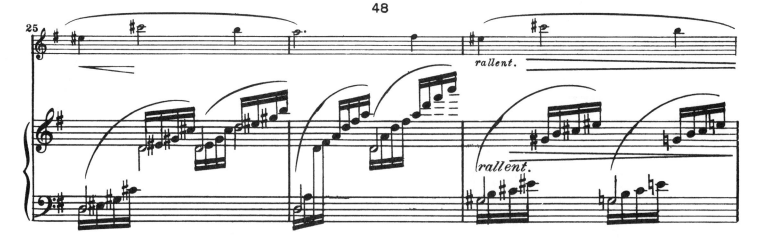

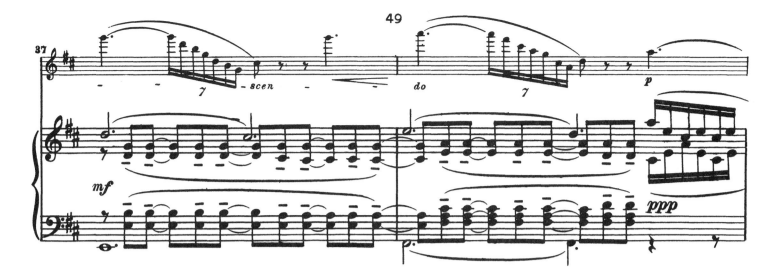

1er Mouvt plus vite que le 12/8
(Tempo I, faster than 12/8)

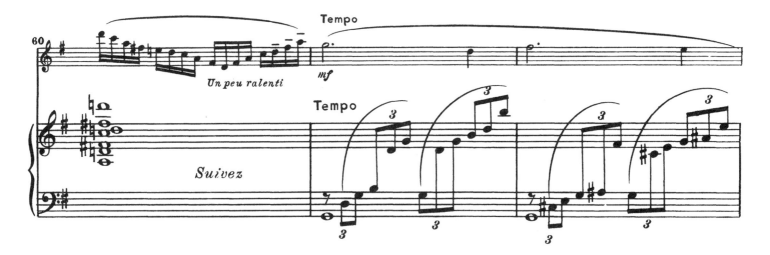

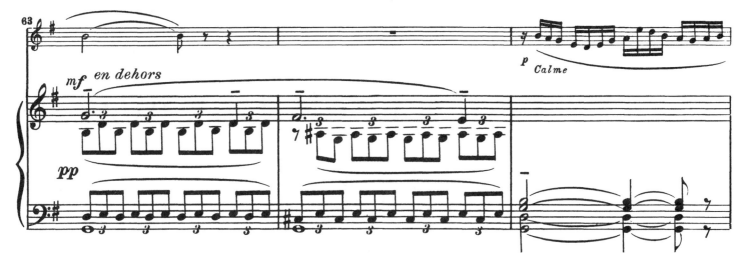

Flight of the Bumblebee

from
The Legend of the Czar Sultan

N. RIMSKY-KORSAKOFF
Edited by H. Voxman

Copyright MCMXLIX by Rubank, Inc., Chicago, Ill.
International Copyright Secured

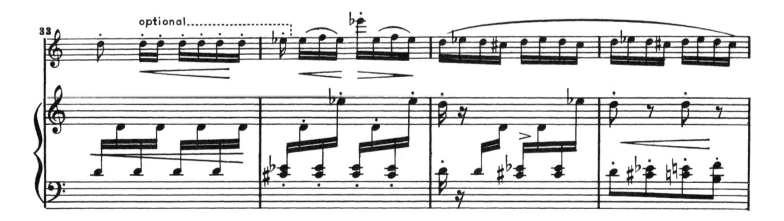

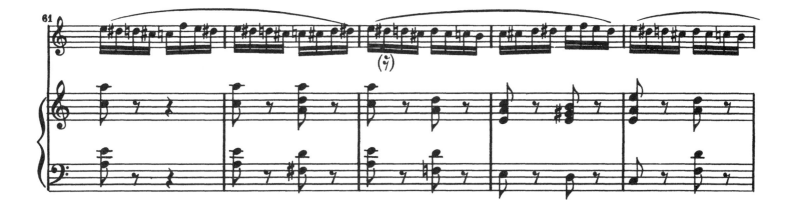

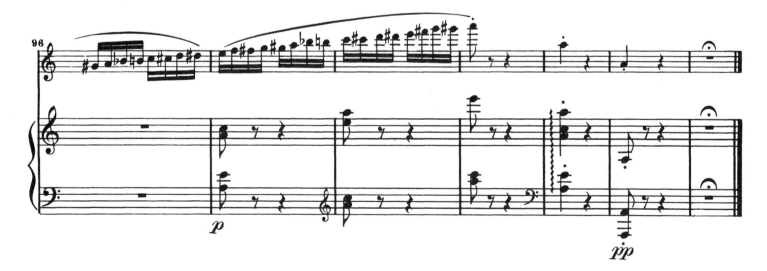

PAN!
Pastorale

J. DONJON
Edited by H. Voxman

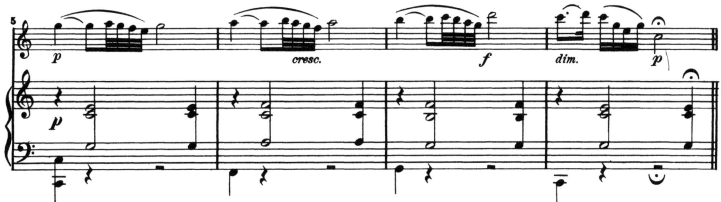

Copyright MCMXLIX by Rubank, Inc., Chicago, Ill.
International Copyright Secured

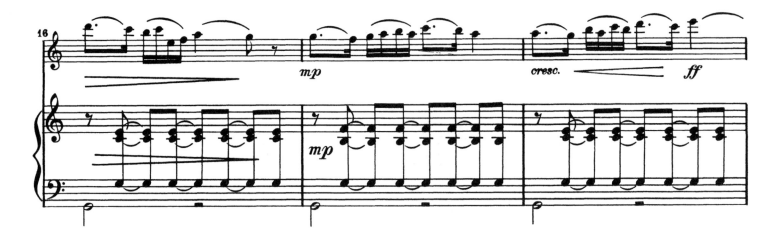

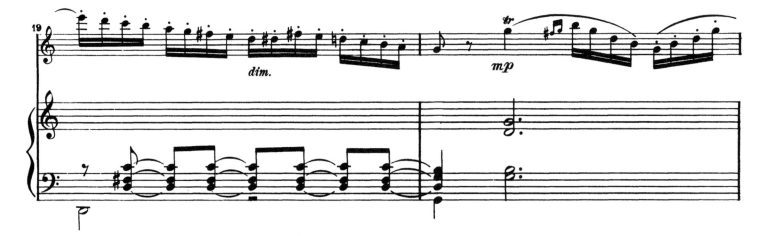

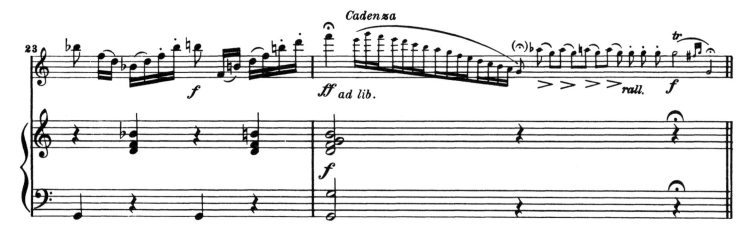